Even

News for every day of the year

Marlene Dietrich in her first starring role, as Lola in *The Blue Angel* (1930).

By Hugh Morrison

MONTPELIER PUBLISHING

Front cover (clockwise from left): Poster for *Anna Christie* (Greta Garbo's first starring role). The R-100 airship. Baseball star Babe Ruth. The Chrysler Building, the world's tallest building in 1930.

Back cover (clockwise from top): Eddie Cantor and Ethel Shutta in *Whoopee!* Ginger Rogers. HM the King-Emperor George V. Amy Johnson. Betty Boop. The Bentley Speed Six.

Image credits: (in order of appearance) Max Fleischer, Ramgeis, Deutsche Fototek, Trish Overton, Felici, Library and Archives Canada, Dominique Salé, Beinecke Rare Book & Manuscript Library, National Gallery of Victoria, Adler Planetarium, F.W. Thiel/State Library of Queensland, Library of Congress, Fanny Bouton, German Federal Archives, Walter Bennington, Mondial/Bibliotheque National de France, Alfred Pearson, Stuart Crawford, Eric Gaba, Galkab, Terence Eden, State Archive of Bulgaria, Walter Mittelholzer, Keystone France, Gan Shmuel Archive, Carl van Vechten, Anthony Kernich.

Published in Great Britain by Montpelier Publishing.
Printed and distributed by Amazon KDP.
ISBN: 9781086767643

January 1930

Wednesday 1: New York City's famous 21 Club opens on West 52nd Street. It has since been visited by every US President except George W. Bush.

Thursday 2: Film director Kenneth Hawks and nine others are killed during an aerial collision while filming in California.

Bonnie and Clyde.

Friday 3: The part-Technicolor musical comedy film *No No Nanette* premieres in New York City. It features the hit song *Tea for Two*.

Saturday 4: The National Automobile Show opens in New York City; the new Cadillac V-16 is launched.

Sunday 5: Notorious outlaws Bonnie Parker and Clyde Darrow meet for the first time in Dallas, Texas.

The Cadillac V-16; launched on 4 January.

January 1930

Monday 6: Australian cricket legend Donald Bradman scores a record 452 not out in a single innings, batting for New South Wales against Queensland.

Tuesday 7: Baseball player Babe Ruth is rejected by the New York Yankees after demanding an annual salary of $85,000, $10,000 more than the Yankees offer him.

Italian Royal Wedding stamp.

Babe Ruth baseball card.

Wednesday 8: Crown Prince Umberto, later the last king of Italy, marries Princess Maria Jose of Belgium in the Quirinal Palace, Rome.

Thursday 9: The Soviet Union appoints US architect Albert Kahn as consultant for all industrial construction in the USSR.

Friday 10: The League of Nations (forerunner of the UN) celebrates its tenth anniversary.

Saturday 11: Pope Pius XI issues a decree condemning co-educational schools.

Sunday 12: 23 men are killed when the navy tugboat HMS *St Genny* goes down in the English Channel during severe gales.

January 1930

Monday 13: The first cartoon strip featuring Mickey Mouse appears in US newspapers.

Horst Wessel.

Tuesday 14: Nazi Party member Horst Wessel, 22, is attacked by communist party members in Berlin and dies on 23 February; he becomes a major propaganda symbol for the Nazi cause. A song written by him, the *Horst Wessel Lied*, becomes an alternative national anthem for Nazis.

Wednesday 15: Five people are killed when communists clash with police in Berlin, Germany.

Thursday 16: British engineer Frank Whittle, 22, submits his first patent application for a prototype jet engine (granted 1932).

Friday 17: Romantic musical film *The Rogue Song*, directed by Lionel Barrymore, premieres in Hollywood.

Saturday 18: Dimitri Shostakovich's first opera, *The Nose,* based on Nikolai Gogol's short story, is performed in Leningrad.

Sunday 19: All 16 people aboard a Maddux Air Lines flight from Mexico to Los Angeles are killed when the plane hits a hill during poor weather conditions.

Dimitri Shostakovich.

January 1930

Monday 20: Buzz Aldrin, the second man to walk on the moon, is born in Glen Ridge, New Jersey.

Tuesday 21: The Five Power Naval Disarmament Conference begins in London.

Wednesday 22: Greta Garbo's first 'talkie', *Anna Christie*, premieres in Los Angeles.

Buzz Aldrin.

Thursday 23: Wilhelm Frick becomes the first Nazi Party member to be appointed to a cabinet-level post in Germany.

Friday 24: Cricketer Stewie Dempster scores New Zealand's first Test century.

Above: poster for Garbo's first 'talkie.' Far right: NZ cricketer Stewie Dempster with fellow player Curly Page.

Saturday 25: Brazilian football club São Paolo FC is founded.

Sunday 26: A civil disobedience campaign begins in India in protest over British rule.

January/February 1930

Monday 27: Grammy Lifetime Achievement Award blues singer Bobby Bland (*I Pity The Fool*) is born in Memphis, Tennessee (died 2013).

Tuesday 28: Spain's ailing dictator, General Miguel Primo de Rivera, steps down and is replaced by General Damaso Berenguer.

Wednesday 29: Archduchess Elisabeth Franziska of Austria, grand-daughter of Emperor Franz Josef I of Austria, dies aged 38.

Thursday 30: Actor Gene Hackman (*Superman, The French Connection*) is born in San Bernadino, California.

Gene Hackman.

Friday 31: Violent protests occur in Hamburg, Germany, as communists agitate for a general strike.

Saturday 1: A bomb, thought to have been planted by Indian nationalists, is discovered in the British Museum, London.

The London *Times* publishes its first crossword puzzle.

Sunday 2: William Howard Taft resigns as US Chief Justice.

Left: looted stores after disturbances in Hamburg, Germany.

February 1930

Monday 3: Michele Bianchi, one of the founders of Italian fascism, dies aged 46.

Tuesday 4: US childrens' educational radio series *The American School of the Air* is first broadcast on CBS radio. At its peak in the 1940s, the programme is heard by over three million children every day across the USA.

Wednesday 5: Sonja Henie of Norway and Karl Schafer of Austria are victorious in the World Figure Skating Championships in New York City.

Thursday 6: The Bank of England reduces its discount (loan) rate from 5% to 4.5% and the Federal Reserve Bank of New York drops its from 4.5% to 4% in hopes of boosting trade.

Friday 7: The League of Nations adopts a resolution to restrict opium growing for medical use only.

Saturday 8: Pope Pius XI publicly condemns the persecution of Christians in the Soviet Union.

Above: Sonja Henie and Karl Schafer.

Sunday 9: Riots break out at Vincennes race track in Paris after rumours spread that races are being fixed.

Right: Pope Pius XI.

February 1930

Monday 10: Actor Robert Wagner (*Colditz, Hart to Hart, Austin Powers*) is born in Detroit, Michigan.

Tuesday 11: The USA and Britain propose the abolition of submarines at the London Naval Conference; the proposal is blocked by France and Japan.

Wednesday 12: The Archbishop of Canterbury, William Gordon Cosmo Lang, attacks the USSR for 'the deliberate putting to death of prelates and parish priests'.

Thursday 13: The British-Indian adventure film *The Green Goddess* starring George Arliss is released in the USA.

Friday 14: The Vatican issues a decree against immodest dress, advising clergy to refuse Holy Communion to women deemed to be inappropriately clothed.

Robert Wagner.

Cairine Wilson.

Saturday 15: US historian and academic William Stearns Davis (author of *Europe Since Waterloo*) dies aged 52.

Sunday 16: Cairine Wilson becomes Canada's first female Senator and one of the first senior female politicians in the British Empire.

Left: Cosmo Gordon Lang, Archbishop of Canterbury.

February 1930

Monday 17: Andre Tardieu, Prime Minister of France, resigns.

Clyde Tombaugh.

Tuesday 18: The planet Pluto is discovered by US astronomer Clyde Tombaugh, at the Lowell Observatory in Flagstaff, Arizona.

Wednesday 19: The All-India Congress Committee adopts the anti-British civil disobedience campaign.

Thursday 20: Prime Minister Osachi Hamaguchi leads the Rikken Minseito party to victory in the Japanese general election.

Friday 21: Richard Luttrell Pilkington Bethell, Baron Westbury, commits suicide by jumping from a seventh storey window in London. His son, secretary to Lord Carter who discovered the tomb of Tutankhamun in 1922, died a year earlier and some attribute both deaths to the supposed 'Curse of Tutankhamun'.

Douaumont chapel.

Saturday 22: On the fourteenth anniversary of the Battle of Verdun, a monumental chapel and lighthouse is erected at Douaumont cemetery to illuminate the graves of those killed in the engagement.

Sunday 23: Silent film star Mabel Normand, a collaborator with Charlie Chaplin and Mack Sennett, dies aged 37.

February/March 1930

Monday 24: Chicago gangster Frank McErlane, an ally of the notorious Al Capone, is attacked in hospital by rival gang members while recovering from a previous shootout; he manages to return fire from his bed and his attackers flee.

Tuesday 25: A bill to decriminalise blasphemy in England and Wales is defeated.

Wednesday 26: Rebels led by General Rafael Trujillo topple the government of Horacio Vasquez in the Dominican Republic.

Thursday 27: Prayers are broadcast on the radio across the USA for the gravely ill former President William Howard Taft.

Friday 28: Spain imposes press censorship and a ban on public assembly to control republican agitation.

Saturday 1: Julio Prestes is elected President of Brazil.

Sunday 2: English author DH Lawrence (*Lady Chatterley's Lover*) dies aged 44.

From top: William Howard Taft. Julio Prestes. DH Lawrence.

March 1930

Monday 3: Ion Iliescu, Romania's first democratically elected head of state, is born in Oltenita, Romania.

Tuesday 4: Over 700 people are killed in severe flooding in Languedoc, France; in Arizona, the Coolidge Dam on the Gila River is dedicated by President Coolidge.

Wednesday 5: London stockbrokers Buckmaster and Moore cause controversy when they advise clients to invest in the USA rather than England, which they say is in 'permanent decline'.

Thursday 6: The first frozen prepackaged food goes on sale in the USA, produced by Clarence Birdseye.

Friday 7: Photographer Antony Armstrong-Jones, Earl of Snowdon and husband of HRH Princess Margaret, is born in London, England (died 2017).

Saturday 8: Thirty days of official mourning are declared in the USA following the death of former President William Howard Taft at 5.15pm.

Sunday 9: Jazz saxophonist Ornette Coleman is born in Fort Worth, Texas (died 2015).

Taft lies in state at the Washington Capitol.

March 1930

Monday 10: 105 people, mostly children, are killed when a fire breaks out during a film showing at a warehouse in the Chinkai Guard district of Korea.

Tuesday 11: The German Reichstag approves the USA's Young Plan for war reparations, agreeing to pay the equivalent of $117bn (at 2019 values) over 58 years.

Wednesday 12: Mahatma Gandhi begins his 'march to the sea' demonstration against the tax on salt in India.

Gandhi (fourth from left) on the Salt March.

Thursday 13: Prolific US author Mary Eleanor Wilkins Freeman (author of *Pembroke*) dies aged 77.

Friday 14: Simultaneous sound and vision television broadcasts are made for the first time in England with an experimental transmitter at Brookman's Park, Hertfordshire. Regular public television broadcasts begin in 1936.

Saturday 15: The advanced streamlined submarine USS *Nautilus* is launched at Portsmouth, New Hampshire.

Sunday 16: General Miguel Primo de Rivera, former dictator of Spain, dies aged 60.

March 1930

Monday 17: Gangster Al Capone is released from jail after serving ten months for illegal possession of a firearm.

Tuesday 18: The British Ministry of Labour releases figures showing that over the previous week the number of people out of work has increased by 15,500 to 1,563,800.

Wednesday 19: Arthur Balfour, Prime Minister of Great Britain from 1902 to 1905, dies aged 81.

Thursday 20: Harland Sanders opens his first restaurant serving fried chicken at North Corbin, Kentucky; he goes on to found the Kentucky Fried Chicken chain of restaurants in 1952.

Friday 21: The Chilean Air Force is founded.

Saturday 22: *Free and Easy*, comedian Buster Keaton's first 'talkie' is released in the USA.

Sunday 23: Maribel Vinson and Roger Turner win the US Figure Skating championships.

Above: Colonel Harland Sanders.
Below: the first KFC restaurant.

SANDERS COURT & CAFE

CORBIN ——— KENTUCKY

March 1930

Steve McQueen.

Monday 24: Actor Steve McQueen (*The Great Escape, Bullitt*) is born in Beech Grove, Indiana (died 1980).

Tuesday 25: The American Federation of Labor releases figures showing that unemployment is at 20% or more in eleven US cities.

Wednesday 26: *Mammy,* the musical 'talkie' with technicolor sequences and starring Al Jolson, is released in the USA.

Thursday 27: Germany's Chancellor, Herman Müller, resigns over disagreements on unemployment insurance for the country's three million jobless.

Friday 28: The Turkish post office announces that all mail addressed to 'Constantinople' rather than 'Istanbul' will be returned to sender. The name was officially changed in 1923 but foreigners were slow to adopt it.

Saturday 29: France ratifies the Young Plan for German war reparations.

Sunday 30: Heinrich Brüning becomes Chancellor of Germany.

Louis Moran and Al Jolson in the hit musical film *Mammy*.

March/April 1930

Monday 31: The majority of US film studios agree to abide by the Hays Code of film censorship. Depictions of nudity, profanity and interracial relationships are banned.

Tuesday 1: The Victorian workhouse (welfare) system is largely abolished in the UK as the Local Government Act 1929 comes into force; some workhouses continue in operation until 1948.

Wednesday 2: Ras Tafari Makonnen Woldemikael (Haile Selassi) is proclaimed Emperor of Ethiopia.

Thursday 3: Mary Pickford wins the 'Oscar' for Best Actress in the second Academy Awards, held in the Ambassador Hotel, Los Angeles.

Friday 4: English cricketer Andrew Sandham scores the first ever Test triple century while in his final Test match against the West Indies in Kingston, Jamaica.

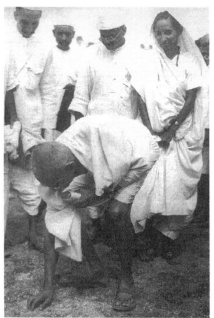

Saturday 5: Frank Digby Hardy, the British intelligence agent exposed by the press in 1920 for attempting to support the IRA, dies aged 62.

Sunday 6: Gandhi's Salt March protest ends at Dandi, as he reaches the sea and illegally boils seawater to produce untaxed salt, declaring 'with this salt I am shaking the foundations of the British Empire.'

Left: Gandhi takes salt from the beach at Dandi.

April 1930

Monday 7: Actor Andrew Sachs (Manuel in *Fawlty Towers*) is born in Berlin, Germany (died 2016).

Tuesday 8: The war film *Journey's End* starring Colin Clive, based on the play of the same name, premieres in the USA.

Colin Clive (centre) in *Journey's End*.

Wednesday 9: Wallace McCain, co-founder of the McCain Foods company, is born in New Brunswick, Canada (died 2011).

Thursday 10: The British Youth Hostels Association (YHA) is set up to provide cheap holiday accommodation for young people, with beds charged at one shilling per night.

Friday 11: Occultist Anton La Vey, founder of the 'Church of Satan', is born in Chicago, Illinois (died 1997).

Saturday 12: Cambridge wins the 82nd Boat Race. With 41 wins to Oxford's 40, Cambridge holds the lead for the first time since 1863.

Sunday 13: 500,000 attend an orderly protest in Bombay, India, against the British salt tax.

April 1930

Monday 14: Indian independence leader and future Prime Minister Jawaharlal Nehru is arrested and charged with breaking the salt tax law.

Tuesday 15: The British Parliament debates proposals to raise the school leaving age in Scotland to 15. Mr FA Macquisten, MP for Argyllshire, argues against the idea, claiming 'children would be much better educated by being out in the open country'.

Wednesday 16: German liberals object to new nationalist prayers for schools introduced by the Nazi Party.

Thursday 17: Mahatma Gandhi's son Devdas, along with 26 other Indian independence activists, is arrested for breaking the salt tax laws.

Above: Mr and Mrs Charles Lindbergh.

Friday 18 (Good Friday): BBC radio news for the first and only time consists simply of 'Good evening. Today is Good Friday. There is no news'.

Saturday 19: The first Warner Brothers 'Looney Tunes' cartoon, *Sinkin' in the Bathtub*, is released. It features the now largely forgotten character 'Bosko the Talk-Ink Kid'.

Sunday 20 (Easter Day): Charles Lindbergh, accompanied by his wife Anne, sets a new record by flying from Los Angeles to New York in 14 hours 45 minutes in a Lockheed Model 8 Sirius.

April 1930

Monday 21: Robert Bridges OM, British Poet Laureate (1913 to 1930) dies aged 85. He is perhaps best known for his hymn translations, including *O Sacred Head Sore Wounded* and *All My Hope on God is Founded.*

Tuesday 22: The London Naval Treaty is signed by representatives of the UK, USA, Japan, France and Italy, limiting tonnage of warships until 1936.

64 British troops and 11 pro-independence fighters are killed during clashes in Jalalabad, India.

Robert Bridges, Poet Laureate.

Wednesday 23: Gangster Al Capone is named 'Public Enemy Number One' by the Chicago Crime Commission.

Al Capone: Public Enemy No.1

Thursday 24: Henry Dudeney, Britain's foremost creator of popular mathematical puzzles, dies aged 73.

Friday 25: Ralph Capone, brother of notorious gangster Al Capone, is found guilty of tax fraud.

Saturday 26: Arsenal defeats Huddersfield Town 2-0 in the FA Cup Final at Wembley.

Sunday 27: The first international radiotelephone call is made from a train, en route from Montreal to Chicago.

April/May 1930

Monday 28: The first regular floodlight night baseball games begin, as the Independence Producers play the Muskogee Chiefs in Independence, Kansas.

Tuesday 29: The first radiotelephone service between Britain and Australia begins.

Wednesday 30: Australian impressionist artist John Russell, painter of the first oil portrait of Vincent Van Gogh, dies aged 71.

Peonies and the head of a woman, by John Russell, 1887.

Thursday 1: US President Hoover tells a business conference in Washington that the country has 'passed the worst' of the Crash of 1929 and that things will 'rapidly recover'.

Friday 2: Grover Whalen, New York City's police commissioner, produces letters he claims are evidence of a Soviet conspiracy to finance riots and strikes in the USA. The Russians later claim they are forgeries.

Saturday 3: The Widnes Vikings defeat St Helens 10-3 to win England's Rugby League Challenge Cup.

Sunday 4: Over 200 homes are destroyed in a major fire in Nashua, New Hampshire.

May 1930

Monday 5: Mahatma Gandhi is interned by the government of India following his salt tax protest.

Amy Johnson begins a solo flight from England to Australia.

Tuesday 6: Approximately 3000 people are killed during an extremely violent earthquake in Salmas, Turkey.

Ace England batsman K.S. Duleepsinhji.

Wednesday 7: Cricketer KS Duleepsinhji causes a sensation when he scores 330 runs in 330 minutes during one day's play for Sussex against Northamptonshire.

Thursday 8: 27 people are reported killed during rioting in Solapur, India, in protest over Gandhi's arrest.

Friday 9: John Masefield, becomes Britain's Poet Laureate. He holds the post until his death in 1967, making him the longest serving Poet Laureate after Alfred, Lord Tennyson. He is best known for his poem *Sea Fever.* 'I must down to the seas again, to the lonely sea and the sky/ And all I ask is a tall ship and a star to steer her by'.

Saturday 10: The city of Sherman, Texas, is placed under martial law following serious lynch-mob disturbances during the trial of a black man, George Hughes, accused of assaulting a white woman.

John Masefield, Britain's Poet Laureate.

Sunday 11: A report by New York's police commissioner shows violent crime in the city to be on the rise.

May 1930

Monday 12: The Adler Planetarium, the first planetarium in the USA, opens in Chicago.

Tuesday 13: Britain's Ministry of Labour announces that unemployment has reached 1.7 million.

Wednesday 14: The National Park of Carlsbad Caverns, New Mexico, is established.

Thursday 15: Ellen Church, 25, becomes the world's first female flight attendant, on a 20 hour United Airlines flight from San Francisco to Chicago.

Friday 16: The USA wins the Walker Cup golf championships by 10 matches to 2 at the Royal St George's Golf Club, Sandwich, England.

Saturday 17: French Foreign Minister Aristide Briand submits plans for a United States of Europe to the League of Nations.

Sunday 18: The Scottish national football team defeats France 2-0 in a friendly in Paris.

The Adler Planetarium, Chicago.

May 1930

Monday 19: White women in South Africa are granted the right to vote.

Tuesday 20: Sir Oswald Mosley, Labour MP and later head of the British Union of Fascists, quits as Chancellor of the Duchy of Lancaster due to a dispute with Prime Minister Ramsay MacDonald over unemployment policy.

Wednesday 21: British journalist George Slocombe interviews Mahatma Gandhi in jail in Yerwada, India; Gandhi expresses alarm over the violent protests following his arrest but remains optimistic about prospects for Indian independence.

Thursday 22: The USA's first public showing of a TV picture projected onto a screen takes place in Schenectady, New York.

Friday 23: US magazine *The Literary Digest* publishes a poll showing that 40% of Americans favour the repeal of Prohibition.

Saturday 24: Amy Johnson lands in Port Darwin, becoming the first woman to fly solo from England to Australia, in just under 20 days.

Sunday 25: Randall Davidson, Archbishop of Canterbury (1903 to 1928) dies aged 82.

Amy Johnson receives a rapturous welcome in Australia.

May/June 1930

Monday 26: The International Olympic Committee recommends Berlin as the host of the 1936 games.

Tuesday 27: The Chrysler Building opens in New York City. It is the world's tallest building until it is superceded by the Empire State Building in 1931.

Wednesday 28: The BBC Symphony Orchestra is founded under the directorship of Adrian Boult.

Thursday 29: 600 animal rights protestors storm a bullfight in Paris; 17 women are arrested.

Left: the Chrysler Building.

Friday 30: Canadian daredevil William 'Red' Hill goes over Niagra Falls in a steel barrel.

The Indianapolis 500 motor race is won by Billy Arnold.

Saturday 31: Actor Clint Eastwood (*Dirty Harry*) is born in San Francisco, California.

Sunday 1: Actor and singer Edward Woodward (*Callan, The Equalizer, The Wicker Man*) is born in Croydon, Surrey (died 2009).

Clint Eastwood, born 31 May.

June 1930

Monday 2: Sarah Dickson becomes the first woman to be ordained as an elder in the US Presbyterian Church.

Tuesday 3: Italy announces that France has refused a mutual agreement to suspend warship building for one year.

Wednesday 4: Two veteran British soap opera stars are born on this day: Bill Treacher (Arthur Fowler in *Eastenders*) is born in London; Edward Kelsey, best known for playing Joe Grundy in the *The Archers*, is born in Petersfield, Hampshire (died 2019).

Thursday 5: French industrialists warn that new US tariffs on foreign goods (the Smoot-Hawley Act) will trigger an international tariff war.

Friday 6: Following a previous renunciation of the throne of Romania, King Carol II returns to his country and replaces the Regency of his son, Prince Michael.

Saturday 7: Carl Gustaf Ekman becomes Prime Minister of Sweden.

Sunday 8: British theatre producer, Sir Michael Codron, who brought Harold Pinter's first play *The Birthday Party* to the stage, is born in London.

Left: William 'Red' Hill in his Niagra Falls barrel.

June 1930

Monday 9: Chicago Tribune reporter Jake Lingle is gunned down in the city's Illinois railway station; he is later revealed to have had large gambling debts and links to Al Capone.

Tuesday 10: The report of the Simon Commission on Indian constitutional reform is published; Indian nationalists refuse to accept it.

Wednesday 11: The Royal Navy launches three new Rainbow Class submarines: HMS *Regent, Regulus and Rover.*

Thursday 12: Max Schmeling defeats Jack Sharkey to gain the World Heavyweight boxing title at Yankee Stadium, New York City.

Friday 13: Sir Henry Segrave's speedboat *Miss England II* crashes on Windemere in the Lake District. Segrave, badly injured, is rescued and informed that he has set the world water speed record at 98.76 mph, but dies shortly afterwards.

Saturday 14: American comic book artist Sam Grainger (*The X-Men, The Incredible Hulk*) is born (died 1990).

Sunday 15: Seymour Parker Gilbert, agent for Allied war reparations, warns that Germany will have to practice severe financial restraint in future to keep to its payment plan.

Sir Henry Segrave: dies shortly after breaking world water speed record.

June 1930

Don Bradman.

Monday 16: The Dow Jones falls to 230.05, its lowest level of the year so far.

Tuesday 17: Legendary cricketer Don Bradman scores 131 for Australia against England at Nottingham, his first Test century on English soil.

Wednesday 18: Construction begins on the new Franklin Institute museum building in Philadelphia, Pennsylvania.

Thursday 19: The French government condemns the new higher US trade tariffs introduced by the Smoot-Hawley Act.

Friday 20: American golfer Bobby Jones wins the Open golf championship at the Royal Liverpool Golf Club.

Saturday 21: Mexico's Colonel Robert Fierro flies from New York to Mexico City in a record 16 hours 35 minutes.

Sunday 22: Britons Woolf Barnato and Glen Kidston win the Le Mans 24 hour endurance motor race in France, driving a Bentley Speed Six.

A Bentley Speed Six racing car.

June 1930

Monday 23: 150 people are injured in Seville, Spain, as workers clash with police during a general strike.

Tuesday 24: Prison drama film *The Big House* starring Chester Morris and Wallace Beery premieres in New York City.

Wednesday 25: HM King George V attends a service in St Paul's Cathedral, London in celebration of ts extensive restoration following closure for public safety reasons in 1924.

Thursday 26: 30 people are killed when the vessel *John B. King*, carrying a cargo of dynamite, explodes after being hit by lightning near Brockville, Ontario, Canada.

Friday 27: US businessman and presidential candidate Ross Perot is born in Texarkana, Texas (died 2019).

Saturday 28: Carlos Blanco Galindo becomes President of Bolivia.

Sunday 29: Pope Pius XI canonises the Canadian Martyrs, eight Jesuit priests killed while on missionary work in Canada in the seventeenth century.

Chester Morris (left) and Wallace Beery in *The Big House*.

June/July 1930

Wimbledon winners: Helen Wills and Bill Tilden.

Monday 30: The Anglo-Iraqi Treaty is signed, beginning the process towards independence from British rule in 1932.

Tuesday 1: The Allied occupation of the Rhineland ends.

Wednesday 2: Carlos Menem, President of Argentina (1989-1999) is born in La Rioja, Argentina.

Thursday 3: Otto Strasser leaves Germany's Nazi Party and sets up a more moderate party known as the Black Front.

Friday 4: Helen Wills (USA) defeats Elizabeth Ryan at the Wimbledon ladies' singles tennis final.

Saturday 5: Bill Tilden (USA) defeats Wilmer Allison Jr at the Mens' singles tennis finals at Wimbledon.

The Lambeth Conference of the Anglican (Episcopal) church approves the use of birth control for married couples.

Sunday 6: Police clash with pro-independence protestors in Poona, India, as large crowds demonstrate in support of imprisoned leader Mahatma Gandhi.

July 1930

Sir Arthur Conan Doyle.

Monday 7: Author Sir Arthur Conan Doyle, creator of Sherlock Holmes, dies aged 71.

Tuesday 8: HM King George V opens the High Commission for India (India House) in Aldwych, London, as part of long term plans for India to become a self-governing British Dominion.

Wednesday 9: The Green Line coach company is formed, linking London with rural towns up to 30 miles from the capital.

A Green Line bus 1930.

Thursday 10: The term 'asylum' is officially abolished in Britain, and replaced by 'mental institution'.

Friday 11: Germany's high court bans school prayers introduced by Nazi Party member Wilhelm Frick which ask God to 'punish the betrayal of Germany'.

Saturday 12: American golfer Bobby Jones wins the US Open title at Interlachen, Minnesota.

Sunday 13: Uruguay hosts the first FIFA football World Cup tournament.

July 1930

Monday 14: The BBC transmits the first ever television play, *The Man With the Flower in his Mouth.* The 30 minute transmission is watched by the Prime Minister, Ramsay MacDonald, on a prototype television set at 10 Downing Street.

Tuesday 15: The jobless total in Great Britain reaches 1.9m.

Wednesday 16: Transcontinental and Western Airlines begins in the USA. In 1950 it is renamed TWA (Trans-World Airlines).

Thursday 17: Labour MP John Beckett is suspended from Britain's House of Commons after seizing the ceremonial mace during a debate on India. The mace represents the authority of the monarch and Parliament may not proceed without it.

Friday 18: Germany's parliament is dissolved amid a constitutional crisis, enabling the government to rule dictatorially.

Saturday 19: Admiral Richard E Byrd, US Navy, and his crew return from a two-year exploration of the South Pole.

Sunday 20: Monaco's Louis Chiron wins the Belgian Grand Prix.

Admiral Byrd and his Antarctic ships.

July 1930

Monday 21: The USA becomes the first country to ratify the London Naval Treaty on arms limitation.

Tuesday 22: Actor and screenwriter Jeremy Lloyd, creator of the BBC sitcoms *Are You Being Served?* and *Allo Allo*, is born in Danbury, Essex (died 2014).

Wednesday 23: Over 1400 people are killed in an earthquake in Irpinia, Italy.

Thursday 24: 23 people are killed by a tornado in Udine-Treviso, Italy.

Friday 25: The Philadelphia Athletics undertake a 'triple steal' twice in a baseball game against the Cleveland Indians, the first and only time this has occurred in major-league baseball.

Saturday 26: *John Bull* magazine publishes an expose of occultist Aleister Crowley in advance of an exhibition of his artwork in London. The paper describes him as 'the worst man in Britain'.

Sunday 27: Cyclist Andre Leducq wins the Tour de France.

Left: André Leducq.
Above: Occultist Aleister Crowley, described as 'the worst man in Britain'.

July/August 1930

Monday 28: The Conservative Party led by R.B. Bennett wins the Canadian general election.

Tuesday 29: Britain ratifies the London Naval Treaty.

Wednesday 30: Uruguay defeats Argentina 4-2 in the FIFA football World Cup final in Montevideo.

Thursday 31: The pulp fiction hero The Shadow first appears on CBS radio in the USA, with his famous catchphrase, 'Who knows what evil lurks in the hearts of men? The Shadow knows'.

Pulp hero The Shadow.

Above: the R100 airship moored at Cardington, Bedfordshire, England.

Friday 1: The British airship R100 sets a record by crossing the Atlantic from England to Canada in 78 hours and 51 minutes.

Saturday 2: Quantum physicist Carl Anderson discovers the positron particle, also known as 'anti-matter' at the University of California, Berkeley.

Sunday 3: Trolleybuses replace trams throughout most of northwest England's Greater Manchester area.

August 1930

Monday 4: The 'King Kullen' grocery store opens in Queens, New York City. A semi-self service store with cash checkouts and parking, it is generally recognised as the world's first supermarket.

Neil Armstrong.

Tuesday 5: Neil Armstrong, the first man to walk on the moon, is born in Wapakoneta, Ohio (died 2012).

Wednesday 6: New York's supreme court judge Joseph Force Crater goes missing; despite a national manhunt no trace of him is ever found and he is declared legally dead in 1939.

Thursday 7: Two black men accused of rape and murder, Thomas Shipp and Abram Smith, are lynched by a mob in Marion, Indiana.

Left: Betty Boop.

Friday 8: Joan Mondale, Second Lady of the United States as wife of Vice President Walter Mondale (1977 to 1981), is born in Eugene, Oregon (died 2014).

Saturday 9: Cartoon character Betty Boop makes her first screen appearance in *Dizzy Dishes*.

Sunday 10: 16 communists are publicly beheaded in Hankow, China, as a warning to potential revolutionaries.

August 1930

The R100 passes over Toronto, Canada.

Monday 11: Traffic stops and crowds watch in excitement as Britain's R100 airship becomes the first such aircraft to fly over Toronto, Canada.

Tuesday 12: Billionaire business tycoon and activist George Soros is born in Budapest, Hungary.

Wednesday 13: Frank Hawks flies across the USA from west to east in 12 hours 25 minutes, beating Charles Lindbergh's record set in April.

Thursday 14: Actress Liz Fraser, famous for her 'dizzy blonde' roles in the *Carry On* films and other British comedies of the 1960s and 70s, is born in London (died 2018).

Friday 15: Canada announces a ban on most immigration from continental Europe, due to high levels of unemployment.

Saturday 16: The first British Empire Games (later renamed the Commonwealth Games) opens in Hamilton, Ontario, Canada.

Sunday 17: Ted Hughes OM OBE, Poet Laureate and husband of writer Sylvia Plath, is born in Mytholmroyd, Yorkshire (died 1998).

August 1930

Monday 18: Noel Coward's play *Private Lives*, starring Noel Coward, Laurence Olivier and Gertrude Lawrence and featuring the hit song *Some Day I'll Find You*, opens at the King's Theatre, Edinburgh.

Coward and Lawrence in *Private Lives*.

Tuesday 19: The arches of Australia's iconic Sydney Harbour Bridge are completed.

Wednesday 20: Australia's Don Bradman scores 232 against England in the Fifth Test at the Oval, London, setting an overall Test series record of a triple double century, and securing the Ashes for Australia.

Thursday 21: HRH Princess Margaret, Countess of Snowden and younger sister of HM Queen Elizabeth II, is born at Glamis Castle, Angusshire, Scotland (died 2002).

Friday 22: Danish newspapers announce the finding of the mortal remains of explorer Salomon August Andrée, who went missing in 1897 after attempting to reach the North Pole by balloon.

Saturday 23: Three people are killed in Silesia, Germany, as police clash with communists attempting to disrupt a Nazi Party meeting.

Sunday 24: Britain's *Sunday Express* newspaper publishes the world's first horoscope column, as part of a tribute to the birth of HRH Princess Margaret. The article proves so popular that it becomes a regular feature.

August 1930

Monday 25: Actor Sir Sean Connery, the first to portray James Bond on the big screen, is born in Edinburgh, Scotland.

Tuesday 26: Character actor Lon Chaney (*The Hunchback of Notre Dame, The Phantom of the Opera*) dies aged 47.

Sean Connery

Wednesday 27: The first media report of the 'Loch Ness Monster' occurs when the *Northern Chronicle* publishes claims of local fishermen sighting a mysterious 18' (5.5m) long creature in the Loch.

Thursday 28: 50 people are reported to have died across Great Britain as result of a heatwave.

Circled: the tiny Scottish island of St Kilda.

Friday 29: The last few inhabitants of the tiny Scottish island of St Kilda, the most westerly outpost of Britain, are relocated to the mainland over 100 miles away. The last surviving native-born St Kildan died in 2016.

Saturday 30: Investor and philanthropist Warren Buffett, the world's third richest man (as of 2019) is born in Omaha, Nebraska.

Sunday 31: The wreck of the cargo ship SS *Egypt*, which sank in the English Channel in 1922 carrying US$5m in gold, is located after an extensive search.

September 1930

Monday 1: *Escape*, the first film made by Basil Dean's Ealing Studios, is released in cinemas. The company goes on to produce the famous Ealing Comedies of the postwar era.

Tuesday 2: French aviators Dieudonné Costes and Maurice Bellonte complete the first non-stop flight from Paris to New York, in 37 hours 18 minutes.

Wednesday 3: Over 8000 people are killed when a hurricane hits the Dominican Republic.

Thursday 4: London's Cambridge Theatre opens.

Friday 5: Hipólito Yrigoyen resigns as President of Argentina following violent anti-government demonstrations.

Saturday 6: Four Yugoslavians are executed in Italy after being convicted of plotting to kill the country's leader, Benito Mussolini.

Sunday 7: King Baudouin of Belgium is born in Laeken, near Brussels (died 1993).

Dieudonné Costes (right) and Maurice Bellonte.

September 1930

The Eastern Columbia Building.

Monday 8: Two of the longest-running US newspaper cartoon characters, Blondie and Dagwood, make their first appearance.

Tuesday 9: The government of India announces that the demands of pro-independence activists led by Gandhi are 'unreasonable and impractical'.

Wednesday 10: New York's Governor, Franklin D Roosevelt, announces his opposition to prohibition.

Thursday 11: Five people are killed in an earthquake and volcanic eruption in Stromboli, Italy.

Friday 12: The iconic art-deco Eastern Columbia Building opens on Broadway in Los Angeles.

Saturday 13: One person is killed in Berlin during rioting between communists and Nazi Party supporters on the eve of Reichstag elections.

Sunday 14: The Nazi Party increases its seats in the German parliament from 12 to 107, making it the country's second largest party.

September 1930

Monday 15: The closure of 90 railway stations is announced in the UK, due to a combination of the Depression and the rise in motor-bus travel.

Tuesday 16: US actress Anne Francis (*Forbidden Planet*) is born in Ossining, New York (died 2011); singer Glen Mason (*Glendora, Green Door*) is born in Stirling, Scotland (died 2014).

Wednesday 17: Britain agrees with China to build the Canton to Hankou railway begun by the USA in 1904 but never completed.

Thursday 18: The New York Yacht Club beats the Royal Ulster Yacht Club to win the Americas Cup.

Friday 19: The Belgian cargo ship *Tigris* sinks off the coast of Kent, England, with the loss of all hands.

Left: Sir Edward Elgar.

Above: Sir Henry Wood.

Saturday 20: Sir Edward Elgar's *Pomp and Circumstance March No.5* is performed for the first time, conducted by Sir Henry Wood at the Queen's Hall, London.

Sunday 21: Actress Dawn Addams (*A King in New York, Father Dear Father*) is born in Felixstowe, Suffolk, England.

September 1930

Monday 22: Boston Braves baseball player George Harold Sisler, nicknamed 'Gorgeous George' plays his final game, against the Chicago Cubs. His 257-run record set in 1920 stands unbroken until 2004.

Bobby Jones.

Tuesday 23: Johannes Ostermeir is granted a patent for the first camera flash bulb, beginning a new era in indoor photography.

Wednesday 24: 48 'counter-revolutionary' government officials are executed in the Soviet Union.

Thursday 25: Nazi Party leader Adolf Hitler states in the Leipzig supreme court that he is 'committed to legality' and will only take power in Germany through democratic means.

Friday 26: 15 people are killed in clashes between police and pro-independence demonstrators in Panvel, India.

Saturday 27: US golfer Bobby Jones wins the 1930 US Amateur contest at Merion, Pennsylvania, thus achieving the Grand Slam (victory in all four major golf tournaments of the year).

Sunday 28: *Soup to Nuts*, the first film featuring the comedy trio The Three Stooges, is released in the USA.

The Three Stooges.

September/October 1930

Monday 29: Russian realist painter Ilya Repin dies aged 86.

Tuesday 30: The all-talking, all-colour musical film *Whoopee!* starring Eddie Cantor and featuring the hit song *Makin' Whoopee* is released in the USA.

Wednesday 1: The 1930 Imperial Conference, bringing together the eight major countries of the British Empire, begins in London.

Thursday 2: Western film *The Big Trail*, featuring John Wayne in his first starring role, premieres at Grauman's Chinese Theatre in Hollywood.

Friday 3: A revolution begins in Brazil, which eventually ousts the government of President Washington Luis on 24 October.

Saturday 4: The British airship R101 departs on her maiden flight, from Cardington, Bedfordshire, to Karachi, India.

Sunday 5: The R101 airship crashes in bad weather near Allone, France; 48 of the 54 people on board are killed.

Eddie Cantor and Ethel Shutta in *Whoopee!*

October 1930

Monday 6: Australian cricketer and commentator Richie Benaud is born in Penrith, New South Wales (died 2015).

Tuesday 7: Indian socialist revolutionary Bhagat Singh and two accomplices are sentenced to death for the murder of British police officer John Saunders in Lahore in 1928. Saunders, a 21 year old of junior rank, was mistaken for a senior officer whom Singh claimed was responsible for the death of a demonstrator.

Wednesday 8: The Philadelphia Athletics defeat the St Louis Cardinals 7-1 to win the World Series baseball tournament.

Thursday 9: Laura Ingells becomes the first woman to fly solo across the USA, travelling from Long Island to Glendale, California, in 30 hours 27 minutes.

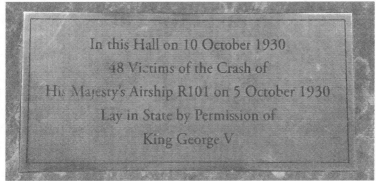

In this Hall on 10 October 1930
48 Victims of the Crash of
His Majesty's Airship R101 on 5 October 1930
Lay in State by Permission of
King George V

Above: memorial to the victims of the R101 disaster.

Friday 10: A memorial service is held in St Paul's Cathedral, London, for the victims of the R101 airship disaster. A half-mile long queue of 90,000 people forms to pay respects to the bodies lying in state at the Palace of Westminster.

Saturday 11: Indian independence leader Jawaharlal Nehru is released from prison after completion of his sentence for defiance of the Salt Tax laws.

Sunday 12: 100,000 socialists hold an anti-Nazi rally in Berlin.

October 1930

Monday 13: Disorder breaks out Berlin as the Reichstag (Parliament) re-opens; Nazi Party members defy the rule against attending in uniform.

Tuesday 14: The stage musical *Girl Crazy* by George and Ira Gershwin, starring Ginger Rogers and Ethel Merman, opens on Broadway.

Above: Ginger Rogers.

Wednesday 15: Chemical industrialist Herbert Henry Dow, founder of the Dow Chemical Company and recipient of over 90 patents, dies aged 64.

Thursday 16: The Reverend Canon John Polkinghorne KBE, theoretical physicist and Anglican priest, (author of *The Quantum World*) is born in Weston-Super-Mare, England.

Friday 17: Dr Robert Atkins, nutritionist and proponent of the Atkins Diet, is born in Columbus, Ohio (died 2003).

Saturday 18: Jockey Joseph Sylvester wins a record seven races in one day, during an eight-race meeting at Ravenna, Ohio.

Sunday 19: Australia's Charles Kingsford Smith completes a flight from England to Australia in a record 10.5 days.

Right: Charles Kingsford Smith.

October 1930

Monday 20: Zionist leader Chaim Weizmann resigns after the publication of British proposals for Palestine which are seen as contrary to the 1917 Balfour Declaration pledging support for a Jewish homeland.

Tuesday 21: 270 men and one woman are killed in an explosion in a mine at Alsdorf, Germany; the second worst mining disaster in the country's history.

Wednesday 22: The BBC Symphony Orchestra, conducted by Adrian Boult, gives its first concert at Queen's Hall, London.

Thursday 23: General Chiang Kai-Shek, leader of the Republic of China, converts to Christianity in an adult baptism ceremony in Shanghai.

Friday 24: Brazil's President Washington Luis resigns in favour of a rebel government following three weeks of civil war.

Saturday 25: King Boris III of Bulgaria marries Princes Giovanna of Savoy, daughter of the King of Italy.

Their Majesties the King and Queen of Bulgaria.

Sunday 26: Australian pilot Jessie Miller sets the female transcontinental flight record, flying from Los Angeles to New York in 21 hours 47 minutes.

October/November 1930

Monday 27: In a speech in Rome about growing militarisation in Europe, Italy's dictator Benito Mussolini claims Italy is only arming itself in self defence.

Tuesday 28: Business magnate and Formula One supremo Bernie Ecclestone is born in Bungay, Suffolk, England.

Wednesday 29: 16 people are killed when a train derails between Geneva and Bordeaux.

Mussolini.

Thursday 30: Turkey and Greece, enemies for many years, sign an accord of friendship and neutrality.

Emperor Haile Selassie of Ethiopia.

Friday 31: Astronaut Michael Collins, who piloted the Apollo 11 Command Module in orbit while Armstrong and Aldrin walked on the moon in 1969, is born in Rome, Italy.

Saturday 1: The Detroit-Windsor Tunnel between the USA and Canada opens. It is the first underground road tunnel to link two countries.

Sunday 2: The coronation of Emperor Haile Selassie takes place in Ethiopia. He becomes an important figure in Rastafarianism.

November 1930

Monday 3: Maxwell Anderson's blank-verse play about Queen Elizabeth I, *Elizabeth the Queen*, premieres on Broadway.

Tuesday 4: President Hoover and the Republican party suffer considerable losses in the US Midterm elections.

Wednesday 5: *All Quiet on the Western Front* wins the Oscar for Best Picture in the 3rd Academy Awards in Los Angeles.

Thursday 6: A man is found dead in a burning motor car in Northamptonshire, England, in what becomes known as the 'Blazing Car Murder'. The unidentified hitchhiker was killed by salesman Alfred Rouse, who was attempting to fake his own death to claim insurance. Rouse is hanged for murder in 1931.

Friday 7: Lenin's Mausoleum in Moscow is opened as a permanent memorial to the Soviet leader on the 13th anniversary of the Russian revolution.

Saturday 8: Professor Sir Edmund (Ted) Happold, structural engineer who helped create the Sydney Opera House and the Pompidou Centre, Paris, is born in Leeds, England (died 1996).

Sunday 9: The Social Democratic Party is victorious in the Austrian general election; no communist nor Nazi Party member wins a seat.

Lenin's Mausoleum.

November 1930

Monday 10: Thirty people are injured when four elephants go on a stampede during London's Lord Mayor's Show.

Tuesday 11: Albert Einstein and his former student, Leó Szilárd, are awarded a patent for the 'Einstein Refrigerator' requiring no moving parts. The fridge is later adapted and produced by Electrolux.

Above: His Highness the Aga Khan III, leader of the Indian delegation at the Round Table Conference in London.

Wednesday 12: The first Round Table Conference between the British government and Indian independence campaigners begins in London.

Thursday 13: German geophysicist Alfred Wegener, originator of the theory of continental drift, dies aged 50.

Friday 14: Osachi Hamuguchi, Prime Minister of Japan, is seriously injured in an assassination attempt in Tokyo.

Wrestler Shirley Crabtree ('Big Daddy') is born in Halifax, West Yorkshire (died 1997).

Saturday 15: British dystopian author JG Ballard (*Empire of the Sun, High Rise, Crash*) is born in Shanghai, China.

Sunday 16: Mihir Sen, the first Indian to swim the English Channel, described by the *Guinness Book of Records* as the 'world's greatest long distance swimmer' is born in Bengal (died 1997).

November 1930

Monday 17: 200,000 workers in Madrid, Spain, join a general strike; a similar strike begins in the country's second city, Barcelona.

Tuesday 18: Pay cuts for government workers take place in Italy; the country's leader Benito Mussolini himself takes a 12% cut.

Wednesday 19: Following serious rioting the Barcelona general strike is called off.

Thursday 20: Germany's foreign minister Julius Curtis announces that Germany may have to delay its Young Plan wartime reparation payments.

Friday 21: General Douglas MacArthur becomes, at 50, the youngest ever Chief of Staff of the US Army.

Saturday 22: Soviet leader Joseph Stalin gives his first interview to a western news agency, refuting rumours that he has been assassinated.

Sunday 23: 31 people are killed when the German cargo ship *Luise Leonhardt* sinks in the North Sea during severe storms.

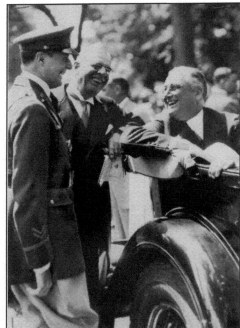

(L-R): Douglas MacArthur, George Dorn (Secretary of War), President Franklin D. Roosevelt, shortly after MacArthur's appointment as Chief of Staff.

November/December 1930

Monday 24: US bank robber Charley 'Pretty Boy' Floyd is sentenced to 12-15 years imprisonment for robbing a bank in Sylvania, Ohio.

Tuesday 25: 259 people are killed in a 7.1 magnitude earthquake in North Izu, Japan.

The first recorded cure of an infection using penicillin takes place at Sheffield Royal Infirmary, England.

Joe E. Brown.

Wednesday 26: 200 students in Berlin, Germany, are arrested after defying a government ban on duelling and possession of swords.

Thursday 27: Germany demands equal treatment in the forthcoming League of Nations disarmament conference, but is told it will still be subject to the terms of the 1919 Treaty of Versailles.

Friday 28: The musical film *The Lottery Bride* starring Jeannette MacDonald and Joe E Brown premieres in the USA.

Saturday 29: Surrealist film *L'Age d'Or* (*The Golden Age*) co-written by artist Salvador Dali and directed by Luis Buñuel premieres in Paris, France.

Sunday 30: Nazi Party members win 32 out of 120 seats in state elections in Bremen, Germany.

Salvador Dali.

December 1930

Monday 1: 75,000 Scottish coal miners go on strike over new working hours.

President Hoover.

Tuesday 2: US President Herbert Hoover gives his second State of the Union address and asks Congress for $150m to institute public works programmes.

Wednesday 3: French film director Jean-Luc Godard, pioneer of the 'New Wave' movement, is born in Paris, France.

Thursday 4: Otto Ender becomes Chancellor of Austria.

Friday 5: Nazi Party members led by Joseph Goebbels disrupt the Berlin premiere of the film *All Quiet on the Western Front* by throwing stink bombs and sneezing powder into the cinema. The Nazis view the film as anti-German and it is later banned.

Saturday 6: The short-lived new London football team of Thames AFC hosts the lowest ever attendance (469 spectators) at an English Football League game.

Sunday 7: In the Industrial Party show trial, five Soviet scientists are sentenced to death (later lowered to ten years' imprisonment) for counter-revolutionary activity.

During an experimental broadcast, the prototype TV station W1XAV in Boston, Massachusetts, shows what is generally regarded as the first ever TV commercial (for a local furrier).

December 1930

Monday 8: Agatha Christie's first play, *Black Coffee*, is well received by critics when it premieres in London.

Tuesday 9: US First World War leading ace pilot Paul Baer is killed when the air mail plane he is flying crashes near Shanghai, China.

Wednesday 10: A bank run, one of several known as the Panic of 1930, takes place in New York City. Crowds of up to 25,000 wait in Brooklyn and the Bronx wait to make withdrawals.

Thursday 11: Following the bank runs of the previous day, the Bank of the United States is closed and taken over by the Superintendent of Banks. Around $550m of deposits is thought to be lost as the bank goes under, about one third of the total amount lost in the Panic of 1930.

Friday 12: A military coup against the monarchy, the Jaca Uprising, begins in Spain.

Saturday 13: The Spanish government crushes the Jaca Uprising.

Sunday 14: Albert Einstein gives an address to the New History Society in which he states 'Peace cannot be kept by force. It can only be achieved by understanding'.

Left: Albert Einstein.

December 1930

Monday 15: Ramón Franco, brother of future Spanish dictator Francisco Franco, launches a rebellion against the monarchy; it is later put down by government troops and Franco flees to Portugal.

Tuesday 16: As part of the Panic of 1930, eleven banks close on one day in North Carolina.

Wednesday 17: British composer Peter Warlock dies aged 36 in suspicious circumstances, thought to be suicide.

Thursday 18: The romantic drama film *The Devil to Pay!* starring Ronald Colman and Loretta Young premieres in New York City.

Friday 19: 42 people are drowned when the Finnish ships *Oberon* and *Arcturus*, coincidentally captained by brothers, collide in fog off the coast of Denmark.

Saturday 20: US President Hoover signs the $110m emergency construction bill and an additional $45m drought relief bill.

Sunday 21: As part of his inexorable rise to power, Joseph Stalin expels the moderate premier, Alexei Rykov, from the Soviet politburo.

Far left: Joseph Stalin. Left: Alexei Rykov.

December 1930

Monday 22: US songwriter Charles K Harris, whose hits include 1892's *After The Ball*, which sold 5 million sheet music copies, dies aged 63.

Larry Stevenson, inventor of the first commercial skateboard, is born in Los Angeles, California (died 2012).

Tuesday 23: The Menemen Incident: three soldiers in Menemen, Turkey, are killed by an angry mob demanding the restoration of Sharia law and the Caliphate.

Wednesday 24: English inventor Harry Grindell Matthews demonstrates his Sky Projector, which projects images and text onto clouds above Hampstead Heath, London.

Thursday 25: British 'wild swimming' pioneer Mercedes Gleitze, the first woman to swim the English Channel, swims seven miles across Wellington Harbour, in New Zealand.

Friday 26: The World Flyweight boxing title bout between Frankie Genaro and Midget Wolgast in Madison Square Garden ends in a draw.

Saturday 27: Construction begins at Clydebank, Scotland, on the new British super-liner, the RMS *Queen Mary*.

Sunday 28: Expressionist dancer Mary Wigman, pioneer of 'dance therapy' and shoeless ballet dancing, makes her US debut at Chanin's 46th Street Theatre in New York City.

Left: 'wild swimming' pioneer Mercedes Gleitze.

December 1930

Monday 29: Italian artist Filippo Tommaso Marinetti, the founder of Futurism, calls for rice to replace pasta as the national dish and for knives and forks to be banned.

José María Reina Andrade is elected as President of Guatemala.

Tuesday 30: The hit play *Five Star Final*, a critique of tabloid journalism by Louis Weitzenkorn, opens on Broadway.

Wednesday 31: Pope Pius XI publishes the encyclical *Casti connubi*, condemning artificial birth control. It is seen by many as a response to the more liberal stance on the issue declared by the Anglican church earlier in the year.

Mary Wigman.

Filippo Marinetti.

RMS *Queen Mary.*

Birthday Notebooks
...a great alternative to a card.

Handy 60 page ruled notebooks with a significant event from the year heading each page.

Available from Montpelier Publishing at Amazon.

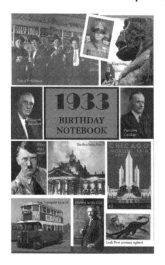

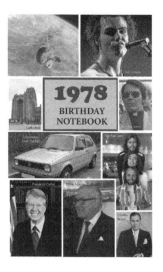

Made in the USA
Monee, IL
27 May 2020